THE
FOREBEARS

1,000 YEARS OF
BEARLY FACTUAL
HISTORY

Illustrated by
Gary Chalk

A DK PUBLISHING BOOK
www.dk.com

Writer and Editor Alastair Dougall
Designer Tanya Tween
Managing Art Editor Jacquie Gulliver
DTP Designer Kim Browne and Jill Bunyan
Production Linda Dare
US Editor Chuck Wills

First American Edition, 1999
2 4 6 8 10 9 7 5 3 1

Published in the United States by DK Publishing, Inc.
95 Madison Avenue, New York, New York 10016

ISBN 0-7894-5349-5

A catalog record for this book is available from the Library of Congress

Color reproduction by Colourscan, Singapore

Printed and bound in Italy by L.E.G.O.

IT WAS DECEMBER 31, 1999, and the Forebear family were
looking forward to their New Millennium party.
"What's a millennium?" asked the youngest.
"A millennium is one thousand years," Grandpaw replied.
"One thousand years is ten centuries. And a century is
one hundred years."
The young Forebears looked puzzled. They knew what had
happened last week, last month, or last year, but 100 years
ago seemed a very long time, and 1000 years ago
completely mind-boggling!
"It's all about history," said Grandpaw, "and my favorite
history is our very own family album. It's full of fascinating
Forebears – explorers, inventors, even royalty – in every
century of the past millennium.
Here are the bear facts about the Forebears . . .

The Forebears' Family Tree

Snapshots from the 11th century to the 20th century

Dolly, 20th century

Bunion, 17th century

Charlie, 18th century

Bruinel, 19th century

Ivan, 16th century

Bertrand, 14th century

Lars, 11th century

Polo, 13th century

Walter, 15th century

François 12th century

Pierre 12th century

A Whole New World!

"EVERYBODY LIKES TO ARGUE about who discovered America. Well, I'll let you into a secret: it wasn't Christopher Columbus in 1492, it was one of us Forebears. One thousand years ago Lars Forebear the Viking looked out from his home in Iceland across the Atlantic ocean and wondered what was on the other side. Following the flight of seabirds, he sailed his longship across the ocean to a place that was later called America. However there were already bears in the woods, and those bears were happy that Lars and his friends didn't stay very long."

The Big Buildup

"OUR FRENCH ANCESTORS were stonemasons. In the 12th century all the nobles wanted houses built of stone, so there was plenty of work for Pierre and François Forebear. But stone houses took time to build, and Pierre and François liked to take things easy. Baron Ambrose Bearpaw promised his wife a vacation home, but when she turned up with her servants, it wasn't ready. Boy, was she mad!"

Welcome to China

"THE ITALIAN BRANCH of the Forebear family produced many explorers. The best known was Polo. In the 13th century, his travels took him eastward to China and to wonderful cities where no European bear had ever set paw before!"

Battling at Sea

"BERTRAND FOREBEAR, one of our ancestors from the 14th century, joined the navy. The Hundred Years War was going on at the time, so poor Bert soon found himself caught up in battle after battle. He was pretty useless at fighting and was always falling overboard. Luckily there was usually someone on hand to rescue him. He used to spend the rest of the battle soaking wet and wrapped in a blanket!"

The big problem with archery at sea is...

...most of the arrows fall in the water and you can't get them back!

Hurry up, my arms are killing me!

How long's this war going to last?

Got him right in the porthole!

About a hundred years!!

I'm getting a sinking feeling!

Gosh, that was close!

There goes Bertrand Forebear!

What is that thing?

Why does this always happen to me?!

Don't rock the boat

Help! I'm at the end of my rope!

Don't you mean "bear overboard"?

Bore overbeard!

Join the navy, they said, see the world!

Read All About It!

"WHO DO YOU THINK invented printing? Johannes Gutenburg? William Caxton? Wrong! It was a Forebear – Walter Forebear – some time in the 15th century. Suddenly reading became the latest craze. The King and Queen were very interested in the new invention, and they ordered lots of books from Walter's little printing business. But setting type was tricky work, and things didn't always go according to plan."

The First Czar

"IT'S A LITTLE KNOWN FACT that the first ever czar – that's Russian for "king" – was a Forebear. He was a distant relative called Ivan, and he ruled in the 16th century. He made the people's lives such a misery with his continual wars, high taxes, and general bossiness that they nicknamed him Ivan the Unbearable. Rulers in those days weren't generally noted for having a sense of humor, but none was more grim and grizzly than Ivan!"

Thanksgiving

"BY THE EARLY 17TH CENTURY everyone in Europe knew there was a whole continent, called North America, waiting to be explored. Bunion Forebear and some friends sailed across the ocean and soon had their very own settlement there. And when they had gathered in the first harvest, they invited everyone in the neighborhood to a feast to celebrate their good fortune. That was the first Thanksgiving dinner!"

South Sea Voyage

"MIDSHIPMAN CHARLIE FOREBEAR always had a taste for adventure. 'Travel broadens the mind,' he used to say. When he heard that a boat was sailing for a new, unexplored continent in the South Seas, called Australia, he couldn't wait to join the crew. He didn't really have any special skills, such as navigation, or scientific knowledge. In fact he was a bit of a dimwit. But he did have a knack for making himself useful. When the ship reached Australia around 1770, Charlie and the crew were amazed by all the new plants and animals they saw."

Speed and Noise!

"MODERN LIFE really began when train power took over from horse power, and most folks went to work in noisy factories instead of on peaceful farms.

Hazey Forebear liked a quiet life in the country; but his brother, Bruinel, moved to the city and became a world-famous inventor. He built an excellent railroad, though sometimes it rattled off the rails! Still, you can't have progress without the occasional mishap."

Moving Pictures

"DOLLY FOREBEAR DREAMED of becoming a star in the newest and most exciting business in the world – motion pictures! She was soon off to Bearswood to make it big in the movies. She was working as a waitress at the Starlight Café when she was spotted by Josef Von Grizzleberg, the world-famous director. He took one look at her shapely paws and gave her a role as a chorus bear in his latest movie. She never looked back! Filming during the heyday of the great Bearswood studios in the 1930s was a pretty exciting business. Sometimes several films were being shot at the same time, so there was usually plenty of action!"

It's Party Time!

Happy New Year

"WELL, THAT'S ENOUGH for now about the Forebear family and their amazing thousand-year adventures. It's time to look forward to the <u>next</u> thousand years. And who knows? Maybe one day you'll help to make history, just like the Forebears. Happy New Year! Happy New Millennium!

THE END

IS NEAR!

**DK Publishing would particularly like
to thank the following people:**

Nick Turpin, Marie Greenwood, and Rebecca
Smith for editorial assistance; Clair Watson,
Laia Roses, and Mark Regardsoe for design
assistance, and Grock Lockhart, Turtle Baruffi,
and Gigio Benfenati for inspiration.

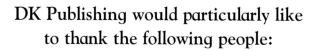

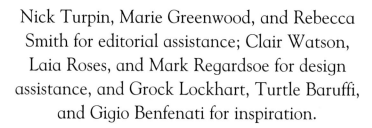